Teacher Tools

by Laura Hamilton Waxman

LERNER PUBLICATIONS ◆ MINNEAPOLIS

Note to Educators

Throughout this book, you'll find critical-thinking questions. These can be used to engage young readers in thinking critically about the topic and in using the text and photos to do so.

Lerner Publications Company
A division of Lerner Publishing Group, Inc.
241 First Avenue North
Minneapolis, MN 55401 USA

For reading levels and more information, look up this title at www.lernerbooks.com.

Main body text set in Helvetica Textbook Com Roman 23/49.
Typeface provided by Linotype AG.

Library of Congress Cataloging-in-Publication Data

The Cataloging-in-Publication Data for *Teacher Tools* is on file at the Library of Congress.
ISBN 978-1-5415-5559-4 (lib. bdg.)
ISBN 978-1-5415-7355-0 (pb)
ISBN 978-1-5415-5650-8 (eb pdf)

Manufactured in the United States of America
1-46014-42931-11/28/2018

Table of Contents

Teachers

Teachers help students learn.

They use tools to teach their class.

A teacher works at a desk.

It holds many tools that teachers need.

What tools might teachers keep at their desks?

A computer is one teaching tool.

It helps teachers plan lessons.

Teachers write on a board.

They use the board to explain new things.

Teachers use books to teach

many subjects.

They also read books to their class.

Flash cards help to teach math.

They help to teach new words too.

What else do you think flash cards can help teach?

Teachers give worksheets to their students.

They give stickers for good work.

A classroom clock helps teachers keep track of time.

It shows when the school day is done.

Teachers teach you something

new each day.

They use many tools to do

their job.

Teacher Tools

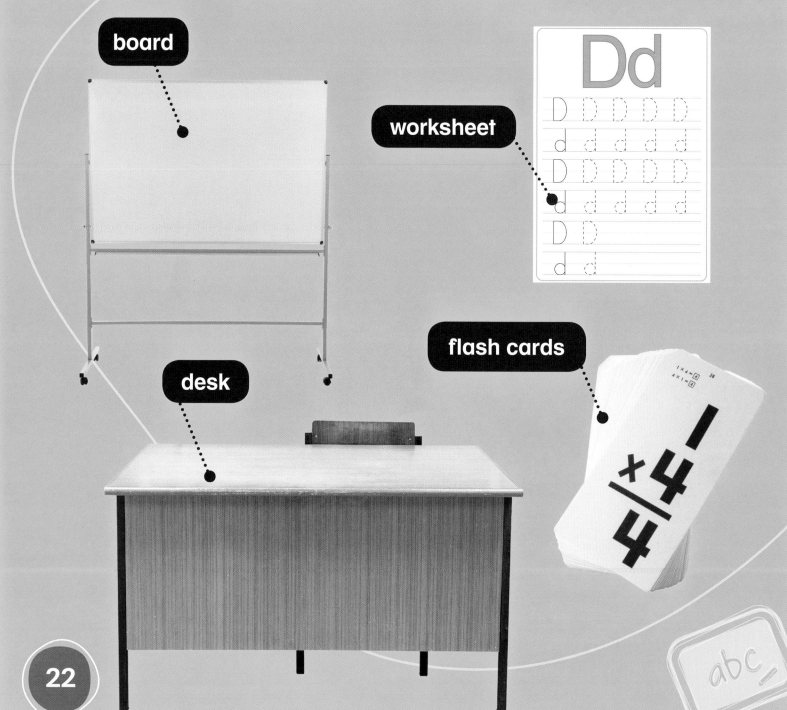

board

worksheet

Dd

desk

flash cards

Picture Glossary

classroom

a room in a school where teachers teach

learn

to gain knowledge

lessons

parts of a subject taught by a teacher

subjects

areas of study, such as math or reading

23

Read More

Heos, Bridget. *Teachers in My Community*. Minneapolis: Lerner Publications, 2019.

Parkes, Elle. *Hooray for Teachers!* Minneapolis: Lerner Publications, 2017.

Siemens, Jared. *Teachers*. New York: AV2 by Weigl, 2016.

Index

Photo Credits